My Pride and Joy. Copyright © 2021 by St. Martin's Press. All rights reserved. Printed in Singapore. For information, address St. Martin's Press, 120 Broadway, New York, NY 10271.

www.castlepointbooks.com

The Castle Point Books trademark is owned by Castle Point Publishing, LLC.

Castle Point books are published and distributed by St. Martin's Publishing Group.

ISBN 978-1-250-27578-3 (paper over board)

Design by Amanda Richmond

Our books may be purchased in bulk for promotional, educational, or business use. Please contact your local bookseller or the Macmillan Corporate and Premium Sales Department at 1-800-221-7945, extension 5442, or by email at MacmillanSpecialMarkets@macmillan.com.

First Edition: 2021

10 9 8 7 6 5 4 3 2 1

my pride and joy

a Grandmother's Memory Book and Keepsake Journal

BY LAURA QUAGLIO

CASTLE POINT BOOKS
NEW YORK

INTRODUCTION 7

CHAPTER 1
Great Expectations 9

CHAPTER 2
Love at First Sight 17

CHAPTER 3
Grandbaby Firsts 25

CHAPTER 4
School Days 43

CHAPTER 5
They Grow Up So Fast 59

CHAPTER 6
Memories Made Together 69

CHAPTER 7
Grown and Flown 81

CHAPTER 8
A Legacy of Love 89

> Children are the
> rainbow of life.
> Grandchildren are
> the pot of gold.
>
> —IRISH BLESSING

Until we hold our first grandchild in our arms, we don't realize how much love our hearts can hold. And when we finally have that love, we want to tell the whole world.

In this memory book, you'll find plenty of places to share your honest thoughts, most beloved photos, and all the little details that make each one of your grandchildren your pride and joy. From the first baby announcement to the last graduation (and beyond), this journal will help you capture your fondest memories of everyone's firsts, bests, and favorites.

When the pages are filled, you'll have a cherished memento to savor in quiet moments—and to flip through with your grandchildren, so they can understand the depth of your love.

CHAPTER 1

GREAT EXPECTATIONS

My Children and Their Partners

How much I thought about being a grandmother before it happened:

How much I shared these thoughts with my children:

The moment I thought my kids were ready to have kids:

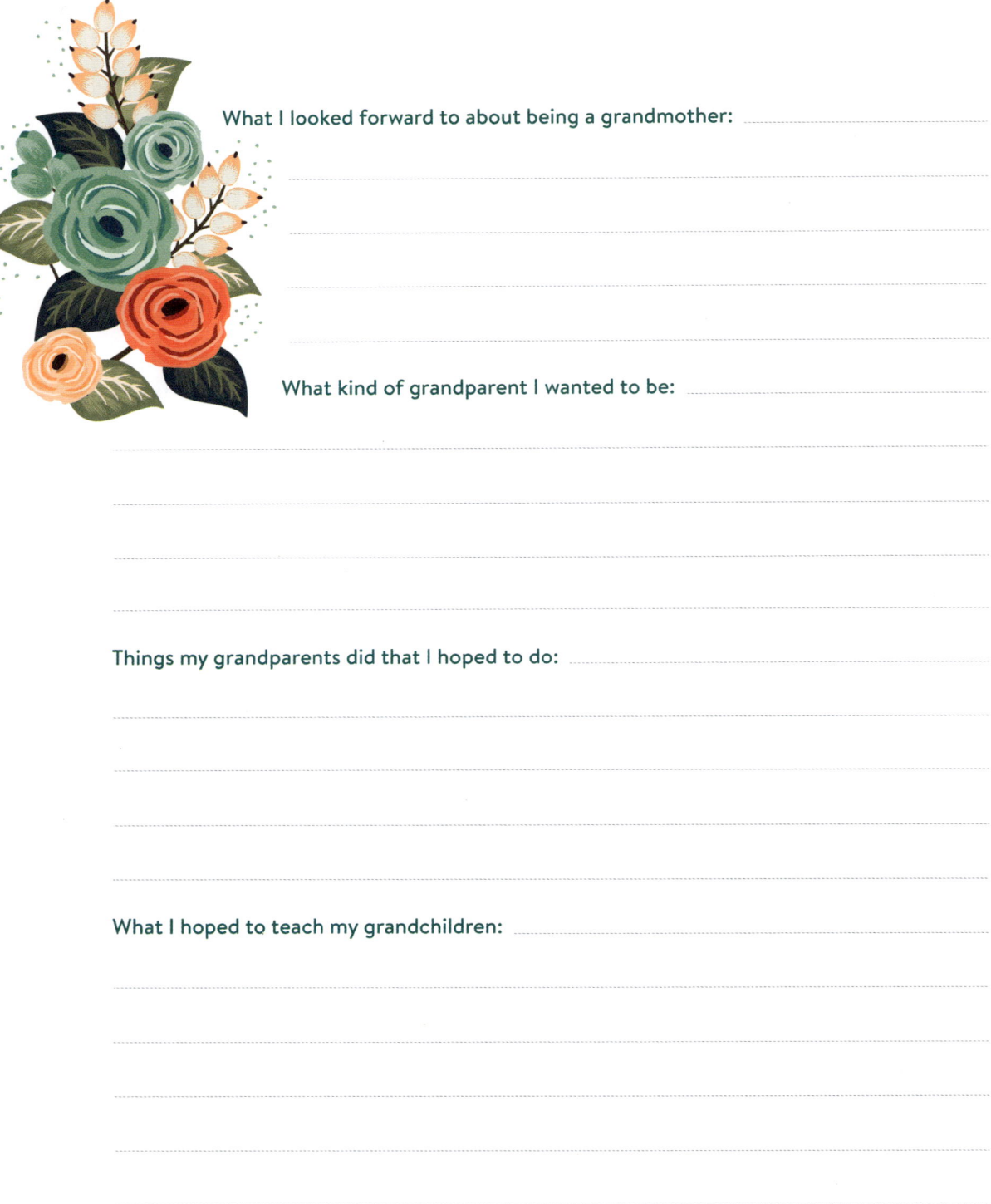

What I looked forward to about being a grandmother:

What kind of grandparent I wanted to be:

Things my grandparents did that I hoped to do:

What I hoped to teach my grandchildren:

The name I wanted my grandkids to call me:

The name my grandkids call me, and why:

*For myself, one of the sweetest words
I have ever heard is "Nana."*

—ZELDA ROSENBAUM

THE MOMENT I LEARNED I'D BE A GRANDMOTHER

Date:

Where I was:

How the news was shared:

My reaction:

How my other grandbabies were announced:

A cherished memory from my grandchildren's baby showers:

Best baby shower gifts I've given:

BEST ADVICE FOR EXPECTANT GRANDMAS:

CHAPTER 2
LOVE AT FIRST SIGHT

Meet My Grandkids: My Pride & Joy

FULL NAME:

Nicknames:

Birthday:

Who they take after:

Best qualities:

ONE OF OUR FIRST PHOTOS TOGETHER:

Approximate date:

> **Perfect love sometimes does not come till the first grandchild.**
> —WELSH PROVERB

FULL NAME: _____

Nicknames: _____

Birthday: _____

Who they take after: _____

Best qualities: _____

_____

_____

ONE OF OUR FIRST PHOTOS TOGETHER:

Approximate date: _____

FULL NAME: _____

Nicknames: _____

Birthday: _____

Who they take after: _____

Best qualities: _____

_____

_____

ONE OF OUR FIRST PHOTOS TOGETHER:

Approximate date: _____

FULL NAME: ....

Nicknames: ....

Birthday: ....

Who they take after: ....

Best qualities: ....

....

....

ONE OF OUR FIRST PHOTOS TOGETHER:

Approximate date: ....

FULL NAME:

Nicknames:

Birthday:

Who they take after:

Best qualities:

ONE OF OUR FIRST PHOTOS TOGETHER:

Approximate date:

When a child is born, so are grandmothers.
—JUDITH LEVY

FULL NAME: _____

Nicknames: _____

Birthday: _____

Who they take after: _____

Best qualities: _____

_____

_____

ONE OF OUR FIRST PHOTOS TOGETHER:

Approximate date: _____

CHAPTER 3

GRANDBABY FIRSTS

On the Move

How and when my grandkids learned to walk:

What I love about this stage:

A funny story about their first steps:

How I felt when they first ran into my arms:

EACH ONE IS UNIQUE

Preferred to be carried or strolled:

Wriggled to be put down:

Fast on his or her feet:

Got into the most trouble as a toddler:

Talking Up a Storm

How my grandkids communicated before they could talk:

Some of the first words I heard them say:

How they pronounced my name:

The cutest things I heard them say:

EACH ONE IS UNIQUE

Babbled nonstop:

Quiet as a mouse:

Early talker:

Still as chatty as ever:

Care & Feeding

Childcare skills that came back instinctively:

Things I had to learn all over again:

Best way to get babies to eat:

Best trick to help babies fall asleep:

Notes on my first grandbaby-sitting session:

EACH ONE IS UNIQUE

Most enthusiastic eater:

Pickiest eater:

Good sleeper:

Resisted naptime and bedtime:

Love in All Seasons

Spring memories and traditions:

Summer memories and traditions:

Fall memories and traditions:

Winter memories and traditions:

If I had known how wonderful it would be to have grandchildren, I'd have had them first.

—LOIS WYSE

Adventure Time

First overnight trip to grandma's house:

The museums, parks, and playgrounds we visit the most:

Family vacations I've taken with my grandchildren:

Location   Date

What we did:

Location   Date

What we did:

Location   Date

What we did:

Happy Birthday, Baby!

Cutest, funniest, birthday moments:

Best party ideas and themes:

Gifts that were a big hit:

Another year old!

The birthday boy or girl: _____

Date: _____

The birthday boy or girl: _____

Date: _____

I like to do nice things for my grandchildren, like buy them those toys I've always wanted to play with.

—GENE PERRET

The birthday boy or girl: _____
Date: _____

The birthday boy or girl: _____
Date: _____

The birthday boy or girl: _____
Date: _____

The birthday boy or girl: _____
Date: _____

My First (Grand) Mother's Day

Where we celebrated:

Who I celebrated with:

What makes my child a good parent:

PHOTOS OF ME AND MY CHILDREN

No Matter How Far

How often I see my grandkids:

How often we talk on the phone:

What we talk about:

When I've missed them most:

Grandmothers are people who take delight in hearing babies breathing into the telephone.

Off to Preschool

Where my grandchildren went to preschool:

Head of the Class

What they excelled at:

What they liked most about preschool:

Times when I visited or picked them up from school:

My Toddler Brag Book

Name: _____
Year: _____

Name: _____
Year: _____

Name: _____
Year: _____

Name: _____
Year: _____

A grandmother is a little bit parent, a little bit teacher, and a little bit best friend.

Name: _____
Year: _____

Name: _____
Year: _____

Grandkids in the Spotlight

Performances and Ceremonies

GRANDCHILD	EVENT	YEAR

Proud Preschool Moment

World-Class Grade-Schoolers

Where my grandchildren went to elementary school:

HEAD OF THE CLASS

How they stood out from the rest:

What they liked most about elementary school:

Times when I visited or picked them up from school:

Grandkids in the Spotlight

Performances and Ceremonies

GRANDCHILD	EVENT	YEAR

Proud Primary School Moment

Primary School Photos

Name: _____
Year: _____

Name: _____
Year: _____

Name: _____
Year: _____

Name: _____
Year: _____

Name: _____   Name: _____
Year: _____   Year: _____

EACH ONE IS UNIQUE

The math whiz: _____

The mad scientist: _____

The bookworm: _____

The social butterfly: _____

The artistic genius: _____

Even more to love about them: _____
_____
_____

Grandma's All-Star Kids

Name:

Sport(s) played:

Proudest moment:

Name:

Sport(s) played:

Proudest moment:

Name:

Sport(s) played:

Proudest moment:

A grandma remembers all of your accomplishments and forgets all of your mistakes.

Name: _____

Sport(s) played: _____

_____

Proudest moment: _____

_____

_____

Name: _____

Sport(s) played: _____

_____

Proudest moment: _____

_____

_____

Name: _____

Sport(s) played: _____

_____

Proudest moment: _____

_____

_____

Early Talents

Name: ....

Talents: ....

....

Proudest moment: ....

....

....

....

Name: ....

Talents: ....

....

Proudest moment: ....

....

....

....

Name: ....

Talents: ....

....

Proudest moment: ....

....

Name:

Talents:

Proudest moment:

Name:

Talents:

Proudest moment:

Name:

Talents:

Proudest moment:

First Masterpieces

Drawings and cards that are dear to me

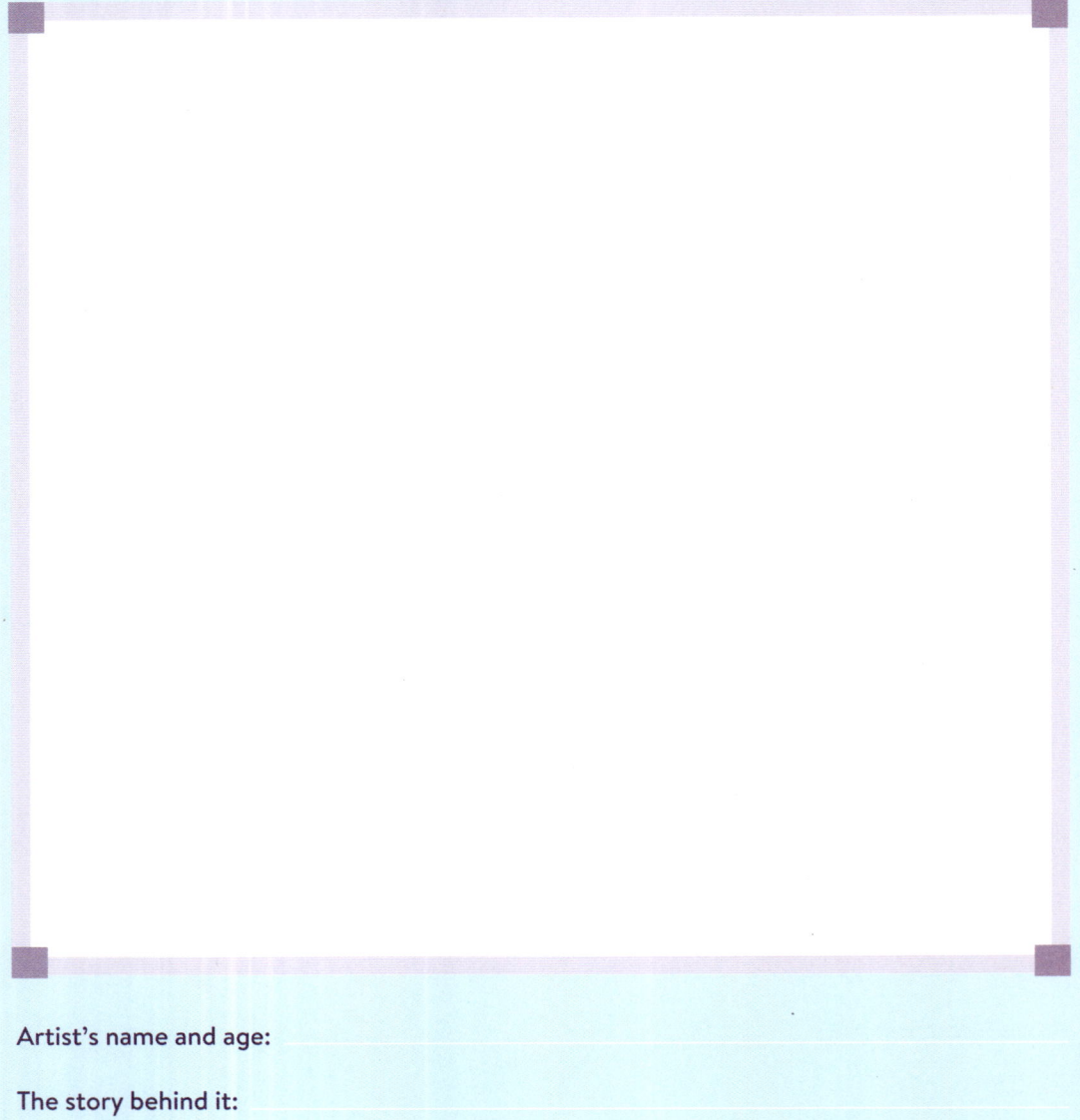

Artist's name and age:

The story behind it:

***God's most precious art is the warmth
and love of a grandchild's heart.***

Artist's name and age:

The story behind it:

CHAPTER 5

THEY GROW UP SO FAST

The Tween & Teen Years

What I loved most about these years:

Changes I saw in them:

How we connected:

TECHNOLOGY THEY TAUGHT ME ABOUT:

Moments I was proud of their independence:

ME AND MY TWEEN AND TEEN GRANDKIDS:

Few things are more satisfying than seeing your children have teenagers of their own.

Emerging Personalities

NAME AND AGE:

Best quality:

Who they take after:

NAME AND AGE:

Best quality:

Who they take after:

NAME AND AGE:

Best quality:

Who they take after:

NAME AND AGE:

Best quality:

Who they take after:

NAME AND AGE:

Best quality:

Who they take after:

NAME AND AGE:

Best quality:

Who they take after:

*Grandchildren are like snowflakes...
each one is beautifully unique.*

High School Years

Where my grandchildren went to high school:

How they are similar to or different from their mom/dad at this age:

HEAD OF THE CLASS

How they stood out from the rest:

What they liked most about high school:

Times when I visited their school(s):

Grandkids in the Spotlight

Performances and Ceremonies

GRANDCHILD	EVENT	YEAR

Proud High School Moments

CHAPTER 6

MEMORIES MADE TOGETHER

What Happens at Nana's Stays at Nana's

How I spoil my grandkids (in the best way):

_____
_____
_____
_____
_____
_____
_____
_____

Rules my children had for their kids . . . that I broke:

_____
_____
_____
_____
_____
_____
_____
_____

Ways I made my home more grandkid-friendly:

Ways I'm less strict as a grandmother than as a mother:

*I don't spoil my grandkids.
I'm just very accommodating.*

Bonding and Learning Together

Things my grandkids make more fun:

Our inside jokes and stories:

New things I tried because of my grandkids:

Skills I helped teach them:

EACH ONE IS UNIQUE

My top chef:

My tech support:

My yard worker:

My chore helper:

My favorite lazybones:

My C.E.O.:

Never help a child with a task at which she feels she can succeed.
—MARIA MONTESSORI

Fun & Games

Favorite card games and board games:

Favorite yard games:

TV shows and movies we watch(ed) together:

Books we've read together:

The laughter of my grandkids is music to my heart.

Games we made up together:

Music we we liked to share:

To Grandma's House We Go

PHOTO FROM A RECENT VISIT

Time Well Spent

Times when I saw all my grandkids at once:

How it makes me feel:

One of the best things in life is when you hug a grandchild and they hug you back even tighter.

Our Special Bond

GRANDCHILD:

Our shared interests:

GRANDCHILD:

Our shared interests:

GRANDCHILD:

Our shared interests:

GRANDCHILD:

Our shared interests:

GRANDCHILD:

Our shared interests:

GRANDCHILD:

Our shared interests:

Lessons Shared, Lessons Learned

GRANDCHILD:

What they taught me:

What I taught them:

GRANDCHILD:

What they taught me:

What I taught them:

GRANDCHILD:

What they taught me:

What I taught them:

GRANDCHILD:

What they taught me:

What I taught them:

GRANDCHILD:

What they taught me:

What I taught them:

GRANDCHILD:

What they taught me:

What I taught them:

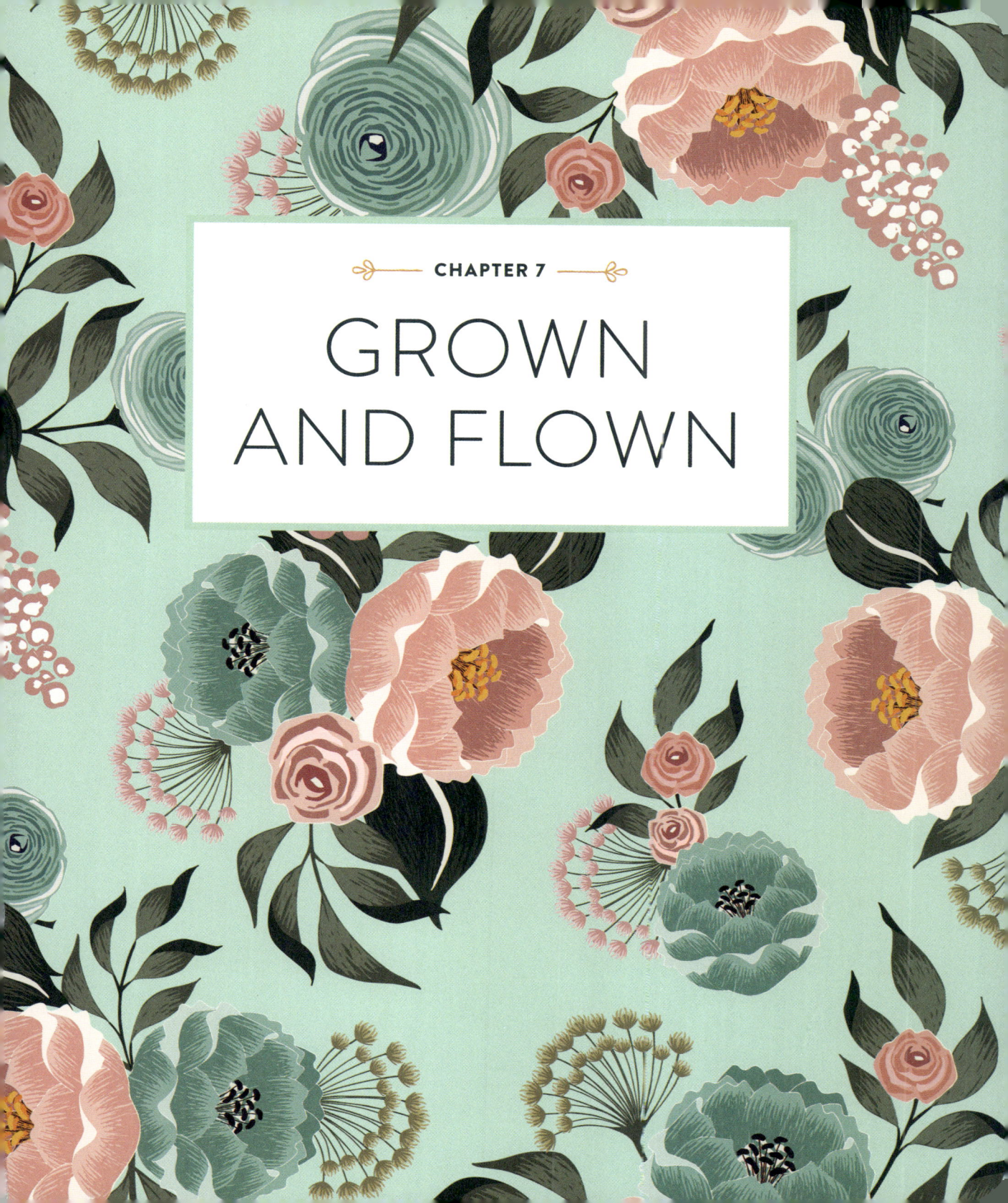

CHAPTER 7
GROWN AND FLOWN

Gallery of Graduates

Name: _____
Year: _____
My Wish for Them: _____

Name: _____
Year: _____
My Wish for Them: _____

Name: _____
Year: _____
My Wish for Them: _____

Name: _____
Year: _____
My Wish for Them: _____

**Grandchildren may outgrow your lap,
but they will never outgrow your heart.**

Name: _____
Year: _____
My Wish for Them: _____

Name: _____
Year: _____
My Wish for Them: _____

Still Bragging After All These Years

NAME: _____

First "real" job: _____

First apartment or home: _____

Goals and dreams: _____

Why I'm proud of them as an adult: _____

_____

NAME: _____

First "real" job: _____

First apartment or home: _____

Goals and dreams: _____

Why I'm proud of them as an adult: _____

_____

NAME: _____

First "real" job: _____

First apartment or home: _____

Goals and dreams: _____

Why I'm proud of them as an adult: _____

_____

NAME: ....

First "real" job: ....

First apartment or home: ....

Goals and dreams: ....

Why I'm proud of them as an adult: ....

....

NAME: ....

First "real" job: ....

First apartment or home: ....

Goals and dreams: ....

Why I'm proud of them as an adult: ....

....

NAME: ....

First "real" job: ....

First apartment or home: ....

Goals and dreams: ....

Why I'm proud of them as an adult: ....

....

Grandchildren complete life's circle of love.

Down the Aisle

Grandchild's name:

Their partner's name:

Ceremony date:

A joyful memory from their wedding:

Grandchild's name:

Their partner's name:

Ceremony date:

A joyful memory from their wedding:

Grandchild's name:

Their partner's name:

Ceremony date:

A joyful memory from their wedding:

Grandchild's name:

Their partner's name:

Ceremony date:

A joyful memory from their wedding:

Grandchild's name:

Their partner's name:

Ceremony date:

A joyful memory from their wedding:

Grandchild's name:

Their partner's name:

Ceremony date:

A joyful memory from their wedding:

CHAPTER 8

A LEGACY OF LOVE

Reflections

Times when my grandchildren needed me most:

Times when I needed my grandchildren most:

Enjoyable conversations we've shared:

How I hope the world changes for them:

How I hope they'll change the world:

Learn from yesterday, live for today, hope for tomorrow.
—ALBERT EINSTEIN

For Keeps

Recipes I'd like to share with my grandchildren:

Heirlooms and precious items I'm keeping for them:

The great use of life is to spend it for something that will outlast it.

—WILLIAM JAMES

Memories I want my grandchildren to keep:

ONE OF MANY DAYS I LOOK BACK ON FONDLY:

Wisdom to Share

Wisdom I'd like to pass on about . . .

Family

Love and Marriage

Difficult Times

Work and Career Success

Aging

*Grandchildren are the gifts of yesterday,
the pride of today, and the joy of tomorrow.*

Bright Future

Things I plan on doing or seeing with my grandchildren:

Moments in their lives I can't wait to witness:

Altogether Now

MY FAVORITE PHOTOS OF ME AND MY GRANDCHILDREN